John Owen

The Retrospect

Or Reflections on the State of Religion and Politics in France and Great

Britain

John Owen

The Retrospect
Or Reflections on the State of Religion and Politics in France and Great Britain

ISBN/EAN: 9783337078188

Printed in Europe, USA, Canada, Australia, Japan

Cover: Foto ©Suzi / pixelio.de

More available books at **www.hansebooks.com**

THE
RETROSPECT;

OR,

REFLECTIONS

O N

The State of Religion and Politics

I N

FRANCE AND GREAT BRITAIN.

By the Rev. JOHN OWEN, *A. M.*

FELLOW OF CORPUS-CHRISTI COLLEGE, CAMBRIDGE.

———————

Atque utinam Refpublica feliffet *quo ceperat flatu*; nec in homines non tam *commutandarum* rerum quam *evertendarum* cupidos incidiffet.

Cic. Off. lib. 2.

———————

LONDON:
PRINTED FOR T. CADELL, IN THE STRAND.

1794.

ADVERTISEMENT.

THE following Remarks owe their exiſtence to ſome of the late tranſactions in that infatuated country againſt which our arms are now carried. The Author was of the number of thoſe who admired with enthuſiaſm the Reformation of the French Monarchy, by the events of the firſt Revolution.— Having had opportunities of obſerving the country at the very diſſimilar periods of July 1790 and September 1793, he received im-

preſſions

preffions of a very oppofite nature, and finds motives of abhorrence to the *later* Revolutions in the principles that led him to applaud the *firft*. The Reflections which enfue were written with no ftudied attention to method, and were dictated by no influence but that of conviction : they are fent into the world in their imperfect ftate, left the delays neceffary to render them more worthy of the public patronage fhould preclude the ufes they are intended to ferve. It was judged unneceffary to crowd the pages with references to facts, as the records of thefe are in the hands and recollection of every one. If it be afked, to what *Party*

the

the Author belongs; he can only reply, That the fpirit of his fyftem is to *fear God*, to *honour the King*, and to *love the Brotherhood*; and that, zealous to fupport the *dignity* of his *Profeſſion*, the *authority* of his *Sovereign*, and the *rights* of his *Fellow-fubjects*, he acknowledges *no Party* where thefe principles are not revered.

DEC. 23, 1793.

THE

THE RETROSPECT,

&c. &c.

AT a period when a people, once renowned for loyalty and refinement, are trampling under foot the rights of monarchy and the fenfibilities of nature; when unconciliated by vengeful regicide they are demolifhing the altars of chriftian adoration, and fanctioning, by acts of ufurped Legiflation, the moft outrageous blafphemies againft the God of heaven: at a period when the profeffional fupporters of eftablifhed devotion are immolating at the altars of reviving paganifm all the diftinctions of revealed religion, — it becomes the duty of all, upon whofe fervices the public have any claim, to oppofe the advances of that enthufiafin which threatens to overfpread the world with unexampled barbarifm.

Fore-

Foremoſt in the rank of human inſtructors
the public teachers of Chriſtianity ſhould feel
themſelves particularly called upon to erect a
barrier in ſuch a criſis, againſt the threatened
univerſality of infidel ſcepticiſm; and in moments of ſuch danger to crowd around the tottering altars of national religion. To *them* are
profeſſedly committed the faithful oracles of regenerative truth—with *them* is lodged the
powerful artillery of chriſtian defence—from
them the public is taught to expect the generous effuſions of inſtructive eloquence, and
the uſeful corroboratives of exemplary faith.—
Conſtituted by the original laws of the empire,
guardians of the public manners, it is theirs to
watch with active jealouſy every departure
from acknowledged rectitude; to anticipate the
conſequences of infant hereſies, and to protect
the fabric of national faith from the aſſaults of
profanenefs, and the ambuſh of ſophiſtry.

The Hiſtory of the World preſents no æra
in which the very exiſtence of religion was ſo
formidably threatened. In all the viciſſitudes
of pagan empire, regard was had to eſtabliſhed
devotion; and protection extended to the altars
of the Gods:—whatever changes were introduced

into

into their modes of government; whatever refinements into their fyftems of faith, ftill the
propriety of religious adoration remained un-
queftioned; and the jurifdiction of the Deities
was confidered as paramount to the threats of
the conqueror, or the decrees of the Legiflator.

In the annals of paft times, the hand of reform has not unfrequently been ftretched to
heal the maladies of an unfound government:—
orders once confecrated by public admiration
have been annihilated, and the idolized diftinctions of a long antiquity have been configned to oblivion, or to change:—yet in all
the havock which fuch comprehenfive regulations
have produced; amidft all the tumult of war,
the rapacity of plunder, and the convulfions of
Revolution, the temples of the gods have ftood
fecure from facrilegious violence; or, if fpoiled
of their votive treafures in the moment of vic-
torious infolence, they have fuffered more from
the enthufiafm of conqueft than the effrontery
of atheifm, and yielded rather to the thirft
of pillage than the wantonnefs of infidelity.

It was, indeed, referved for a nation in the
decline of her political greatnefs, and in the
prof-

profpect of gathering calamities, to exhibit enormities againft Heaven and good faith, which the
moft extravagant legends of fabulous romance
have never recorded;—it was referved for a
nation whofe dawning Freedom aftonifhed the
wife, captivated the generous, and conciliated
the bigotted, to tarnifh the luftre of her regenerated policy by acts of Legiflation, and
events of private example, which kindle refentment in the breaft of Freedom, and fhock
the fenfibilities of the *Patriot* and the *Chriftian.*

It is impoffible to turn the eye of attention
upon the recent extravagancies of the French
Republic, without recoiling at the fanguinary
violence which marks its acts of public authority, and the enthufiaftic iniquity which ac-
companies the individual exertions of its moft
diftinguifhed citizens. By a feries of events to
which maffacre and good fortune, the arti-
fices of faction, and the fatality of circumftances,
have equally contributed, all the happy regulations of a puritied Legiflation have vanifhed;
—a Conftitution formed by united talents and
Patriotifm, has been rudely demolifhed;—a
crude fyftem of changeful tyranny has been
infti-

inftituted, and a handful of affaffins have eftablifhed their thrones upon the ruins of wifdom,
of probity, and honor.

Who, that is not fteeled to the emotions of
mercy can regard with a fteady eye the bloody
progrefs of thofe factious rulers, through all
the ftages of their enormity, from the * day
that opened the veins of bleeding Patriotifm,
and yielded to Republican Cabal the furviving
fpoils of a debilitated Monarchy? Who, that is
not abandoned to fixed infenfibility, can view
with patient fpeculation the laft infults offered
to the fallen Monarch,—the mockery which
affumed the forms of juftice, and the † ferocity which drowned the accents of complaint?—
Warm with the blood of an unoffending Sove·
reign, the fcaffold receives (unexpected furvivor
of the laft indignities) his widowed Confort!—
Perfecuted by all the brutal expedients which
intoxicated faction could devife, fhe is dragged
to that ftern tribunal where juftice frowns in
rigid horrors, and mercy never whifpered foft
acquittal!—All the caprices of paft intrigue,

* Auguft 10th.
† The drums beat when he would have addreffed the
people.

B 3   all

all the tyrannies of revolutionary tumult are rudely charged upon this haggard ghoſt of departed beauty : but councils of intrigue, and fyſtems of difaffection, are not deemed charges of fufficient turpitude to fatiate the demands of greedy malice ; crimes muſt be torn from the abyſs of iniquity, and invention be tortured to imagine faults which may tranſmit to future times the name of Antoinette, under all the black difgrace of unnatural deformity.—But here let the fcene for ever clofe !—Configned to eternal oblivion be the memory of that tribunal which' in exhibiting the laſt triumphs of an abandoned faction, outſtripped all the recorded atchievements of gigantic villany !—Peace to the aſhes of that injured form, which, familiarized by long habitudes to cowardly infolence, were yet called to encounter thofe hideous ſhocks which no acquaintance with practiſed iniquity could anticipate, and which no refources of mental fortitude could fuſtain ! Poſterity will glance with cautious curiofity over this monſtrous fiction of ſtubborn barbarity :—recoiling fenfibility will dread to tear from its drear obfcurity what nature hears not without horror, and what the rifing feelings of the human heart confpire to difcredit.

The

The blow is now ftruck, the monarchy is
fubverted, and the laft fupporters of its declining fplendor have been immolated at the
altars of a revengeful faction. Freedom has
feen, with agonizing throes, the glaring outrages that have been committed under her ban-
ners, and the aggravated crimes which have
covered her proftituted name. All the bonds of
fealty have been broken; pledged allegiance
and covenanted faith have been publicly
violated; and neither the dictates of policy,
nor the accents of mercy have prevailed, to
temper the unparalleled rigours of maffacre and
profcription.

Full as the career of iniquity had fhewn
itfelf, there yet remained a glimmering hope,
that, fick at length of havock and flaughter,
the guilty Demagogues would relax their glutted
tyranny; and the loofened energies of public
virtue refume their intermitted functions :—
There ftill remained amongft the hideous wafte
of demolifhed thrones and abjured divinities,
a ray of expectation, that, urged by frantic
patriotifm to inordinate revenge againft ancient
prejudices, the tide of rebellion would yet be
turned; and the national enthufiafm be dif-
ciplined

ciplined by wholefome and permanent laws.
Circumftances had indeed little encouraged fuch
expectation ; and the greater part of thofe who
had diftinguifhed themfelves by an attachment
to the revolutionary outline, renounced their
affection for a people, whofe inconfiftency had
marred their patriotifm ; and whofe vices had
rendered them unworthy of the public patronage.
There were not, however, wanting amongft the
ftrenuous admirers of the firft Legiflature thofe
who, averfe to defpondency in an affair of fuch
lively intereft, ventured to flatter themfelves
that the nation would revert to its firft principles, and that the fofter yoke of a generous
monarchy would yet fucceed to the oppreffive
bondage of an outrageous democracy. Amongft
thofe who, attached to monarchical authority,
fighed for the reftoration of this falutary fyftem,—
difcordant opinions ftill prevailed ; and the
wifhed-for accomplifhment of this neceffary
meafure feemed to demand, in the view of
different individuals,' exertions of a *different*
nature. To the one, the united hoftilities of
the European powers appeared the only inftrument which could chaftife the infolence of
ufurped authority, and recal to reafon and to
loyalty an infatuated nation : To the other,

the

the gentler maxims of a pacific policy appeared
more confonant with the dictates of public
juftice and political expediency. The reafon
which guided thefe contradictory fyftems
might indeed be unequal, yet the integrity
alike in each. Spectators alone of thefe tumultuous events, each laboured to afcend through
the chain of outrages which fucceeded each
other, to the remote caufes which gave birth to
all. The conclufions were different according
as the refearches had been more or lefs profound, or conducted under a greater or lefs
degree of prepoffeffion. To fome the horrors,
which ftained the later æras, appeared the
defperate fruits which fprung from the co-ope-
ration of internal cabal and foreign hoftility.
To others, the growing ravages which defolated
all the remaining monuments of ancient eftablifhment, appeared the inevitable refult of thofe
early principles which dictated the fubverfion of
political diftinctions ; and infpired the luminous,
yet impracticable, code of human rights.

So novel indeed was the experiment in the
viciffitudes of empires ; fo inftantaneous was
the converfion, and fo rapid the eftablifhment
of this regenerated people, that the moft profound

found fpeculation regarded it with aftonifhment, and the moft difpaffionate philofophy beheld it with enthufiafm. In an event fo new in the annals of legiflation, it were not to be wondered at, that men, equal in underftanding, in loyalty, and patriotifm, fhould have adopted, from the complicated tranfactions, fentiments which militated effentially with each other: It were not to be wondered at, that, regarding the diffolution of ancient eftablifhments, and the fabrication of new regulations, men accuftomed to the freedom of political difcuffion, fhould have had the hardinefs to approve or condemn, as the facts accorded with their received fyftems, or contradicted their habitual maxims of national policy.

The abrupt deftruction of hereditary diftinctions, the bold confifcation of the clerical treafures, the unqualified abolition of feudal privileges, provoked indignant murmurs on the one hand, while they called forth the moft lively applaufe on the other. To thofe who regarded with plauditory triumph the zeal which combated ancient eftablifhments, the ftupendous evils which thofe had produced were prefent in all their glaring extent. To
them

them the hiſtory of paſt crimes was written in blood; and government appeared but a fabricated expedient to plunder and oppreſs mankind, A nation inſulted by an overgrown nobility, feemed, in their view, to demand ſome late redreſs; and vengeance appeared not improperly exerciſed upon peculation, though ſupported by ancient inſtitution; and violence, though ſanctioned by immemorial uſage. On the contrary, thoſe who ſtood aloof, while admiration gazed on theſe brilliant tranſactions, fixed with ſteady eagerneſs on that portion of crime which entered into theſe acts of heroiſm, while they glanced with partial attention over thoſe complicate oppreſſions which gave them birth. Theſe ſuffered themſelves to be engroſſed by the very natural commiſeration of private inconvenience; and made no allowance for that torrent of indignation which centuries of tyranny and wanton perſecution had inſpired. They paid no deference to the exaſperated feelings of a nation, eſcaped from the laſh of guilty authorities. In compaſſionating the few, they neglected to conſider the many; and in the ſufferings of the innocent, forgot the atrocities of the guilty.

It

(12)

It is eafy to fee how oppofite fentiments might enter minds equally difpofed to the fupport of truth, upon a fubject of fuch novelty, complicacy, and political extent. The abolition of Ariftocracy might be confidered by the one, a political good; by the other, a political evil; with a fhew of argument in each contending fcale, that would appear a juft counterbalance the one to the other. In the one cafe, Ariftocracy would naturally find no inconfiderable advocates amongft thofe whom private predilection, added to the fuppofition of acknowledged utility, had attached to its inftitution. Ten thoufand prejudices confpire to rivet the affections to ancient diftinctions; and the mind familiarized to thefe by habits of long and uninterrupted intimacy, affociates the laws which protect their privileges with thofe which nature herfelf promulges. It was natural that eftablifhments of ancient prefcription fhould have found, amidft all their extravagancies, no few defenders; and under all their corruptions, no mean apologifts. The brilliant fervices which thefe have rendered to civilized fociety, the fupport they have communicated in the concuffions of revolt, the dignity they have conferred in the progreffions of refinement,

what

what they have added to the common splendor, what they have operated for the public good, might contribute to commend their fashionable influence, till mankind had forgotten to mark the boundaries between primitive right and covenanted institution ; and learned to blend in one common mass, the distinct authorities of nature and civil society.

On the other hand, the evils that grew out of that pernicious stock, the wild luxuriancy of those multifarious shoots which penetrated every part of the Gallic Empire, had converted this imagined good into a real evil, rendered it an insupportable burden to the groaning subjects of its enormous tyranny, and given birth to disorders more numerous and pernicious than those it was intended to prevent. There is in all institutions of human construction, a point beyond which iniquity cannot extend ; a period at which evil consummates its plenitude, and violence defeats its own purpose. In France, at the æra of the Revolution, aristocracy had found this point. To this crisis had the over-bearing insolence * of the nobles arrived ; when

* *Vide* Rabaud's *Precis Historique.*

senseless

fenfelefs pertinacity urged their extravagance, and infatuated obftinacy precipitated their downfal. It was then, while, intoxicated with redundant authority, and bigotted to diftinctions which were yielding to refinement, they carried their licence to an excefs, which the circumftances of policy and of juftice muft for ever condemn,—that the fparks of a rebellion already ripened, kindled into flame : the exafperated feelings of an indignant people, armed againft the authority of their infulting rulers ; and big with vengeance, annihilated for ever thofe eftablifhments, under whofe licentious outrages they had fo often bled. The blow was fudden and unpremeditated ; particular events haftened on the cataftrophe ; and circumftances, which could not be forefeen, precipitated the meafure. Enthufiaftic with new and unfelt fenfations, the Legiflators of the country were feen to pafs, in the paroxyfms of their zeal, all the bounds of policy and juftice ; they abandoned that experience which might inftruct, for that inftinct which muft miflead ; and, furrendering themfelves to the tranfports of recovered freedom, they fapped the ftamina of their future profperity, tore up the roots of implanted authority, and committed all the props of national fecurity

to

to the raging flames of an extravagant patriotifm.

Perhaps the ruin which has fince extended itfelf throughout the different departments of civil authority, owes no fmall fhare of its prefent magnitude to the unqualified abolition of the ariftocratic orders. The extent of this evil was not promptly apprehended by that zealous enthufiafm which, once embarked in enterprizes of reform, is not ufually confined within the limits of prudent policy. It were, however, eafy to difcover, in retracing the fteps of revolutionary operations, how inconvenient a chafm muft have been created in the fcale of fociety, by the total abolition of orders fo numerous, fo diverfified, and of fuch acknowledged importance in the fphere of authority. In them was annihilated that comprehenfive link, which, in the fubfequent purity of government, would have defined, by an intermediate intereft, the monarch's grandeur and the people's rights; that link, by which the contending advances of the one and the other would have received an effectual correction, and have been preferved amidft all their conflicts in a conftitutional equipoife. The demolition

lition of thefe orders marred the unity of that fyftem which was adopted by the firft reformers, and left a *defideratum* in the future monarchy, which all the energies of patriotic enthufiafm could not fupply.

Amongft the internal caufes of future havock, the abolition of Ariftocracy appears to poffefs the foremoft rank in thofe indifcreet meafures which diforganized the body of the empire, and precipitated the monarch's downfal. The exalted rank of chief magiftrate in an extenfive empire, demands fome medium to tranfmit thofe rays in foftened luftre, which would offend, by their tremendous majefty, the naked fight. The diftance is fo wide in the fphere of created influence, between the throne and the fubject, that all which iffues from the Executive Authority muft, in this cafe, appear to rufh like the cataract from the frowning precipice, inftead of defcending (as it ought to have done) by the mediums of a juft gradation, and circulating through channels of artful communication. France exhibited, in this inftance, an experiment of impracticable policy; and vainly expected from a defective fyftem of garbled authorities, all the brilliant

advantages

advantages of the moft perfect government. But thefe deftroyed, a mighty void was feen in the fphere of government; and the furviving orders were torn afunder by an act of baneful feparation: the bulk of the people were left to gaze, at an awful diftance, upon the monarch, who thus ftood infulated amidft a defolate fphere, once peopled by the fupports of his grandeur and the organs of his authority. A thoufand jealoufies were now feen to obftruct the concord of the exifting authorities, and embarrafs the movements of the executive power.—The monarch faw, with anxious apprehenfion, the bold advances which trenched upon his reduced prerogative:—The people eyed with dread fufpicion, every exertion of monarchical fovereignty, and laboured to confine that power from which they apprehended the return of ancient fervitude. Unfortunately for fociety, all the conflicts which found exiftence between the rival parties, terminated in favour of the populace. The torrent thus acquired force from ineffectual oppofition, till order fell before the formidable engines of diforganization, and the rifing turbulence of triumphant faction acquired the zenith of its influence. Then commenced that fpirit of de-

C   terminated

termined anarchy, which crumbled, in rapid
fucceffion, all authorities, and levelled, amidft
the ruins of extirpated tyranny, a fabric that
had held captive the admiration of Europe.

It would be readily admitted, that the boafted
principles of Gallic Policy (as expounded in
modern fyftems) approaches neareft to the
ftandard of ideal perfection; and that in the
perfection of fociety, a government by reprefentation is not only beft accommodated to
the wants of mankind, but affords the beft
fecurity againft tyranny and corruption. But
the manners of men have not yet acquired their
millennian foftnefs; nor is fociety arrived at that
point of polifhed excellence which is neceffary
to the conftitution of fo pure a fyftem. The
focial virtues of mankind are perfected by flow
and gradual refinements; and all the important
changes which have benefitted the world by
great and durable advantages, have been effected
by patient induftry, and adopted with cautious
policy. To the conftruction of a government,
no mean calculations are requifite. It is not
fufficient that the fyftem be pure, it muft
alfo be apt and practicable.—The tempers of
mankind are varied in a thoufand different
shades;

fhades; they are moulded to different habits by the varieties of climate, of hiftory, and of events; their obedience is to be excited by maxims fuited to their received opinions; and their allegiance to be infured by expedients, adapted to their national chara&er. Refpe&t muft be paid to the extent of their knowledge and the caft of their morals; to the information they poffefs, and the virtue they difcover. In France no fuch calculations were ever attended to; and no fuch circumftances were ever fuffered to have weight. The whole mafs of their revolutionary fchemes was formed upon abftra&t principles of political fcience. All the experiments of paft ages were, by them, held in difefteem; and wifdom appeared to utter her firft oracles in their plans of Legiflation. All their intellect, and all their enthufiafm, were abforbed in imagining fchemes of immaculate policy, inftead of purging the ancient channels of corrupt authority, and giving energy to thofe regulations which had been already ena&ted. The confequences of this fpeculation are now feen; and France will for ever regret the deftruction of thofe civilized diftinctions. Interwoven with the finews of monarchical authority, they drew after them in their fall, that

C 2 ftupendous

ftupendous fabric whof ruinsnow fupport the throne of anarchy and murder.

Whether Monarchy or Republicanifm be moft favourable to general freedom, is a queftion which in reference to the reform of ancient empires, it muft now appear too late to agitate.—Ere the fatal experiment was made upon that country, whofe name now revolts the feelings of humanity; ere the rueful confequences had proclaimed its inexpediency in characters of blood, men might have difcuffed with cool and harmlefs difcerptation a queftion which ftill remained undecided in the theory of politics. But, at a period like the prefent, when ftained with the guilt of unprecedented crimes, Republicanifm is ftalking in giant infolence over the ruins of a demolifhed Monarchy; when, brandifhing a more than tyrant fceptre, it is faftening the chains of unparelleled barbarifm upon the yielding fubjects of its cruel authority; when martyr'd Sovereigns heap its altars, and bleeding Patriots adorn its orgies; when holy faith and Chriftian devotion exhibit their lacerated forms, and fly before the demons of its impious idolatry; when the ancient profeffors of eftablifhed religion are abjuring

juring with public blafphemy the God they
ferved; when the hoary prieft is immolating
his ancient functions to the Baals of pretended
philofophy, and demolifhing thofe altars which
once fmoked with the incenfe of his facrifice—
in fuch a moment, and in the face of fuch enormities, to move a queftion, were to offer an
apology; and not to execrate, were almoft to
approve,

It is admitted, that in the earlier ftages of
their Revolutionary Hiftory, when intent upon
modifying their internal government they ab-
ftained from acts of outrage, the opinions of
mankind might be innocently divided upon the
wifdom and equity of their operations. When
they even arrived to that height of extravagance
which dethroned the Monarch, inverted the
laws, and gave up every valued inftitution
to caprice and change,—nations unconnected
with the confequences thefe drew on, might
ftill regard, without a neceffary intereft, the
progreffive revolutions their authorities experienced; and individuals might ftill comment, as
their feelings or their judgment fuggefted, upon
the events that rofe before them;—but when
big with infolence, or prompted by ambition;

C 3   when

when harraffed by inconvenience or intoxicated with fuccefs, they denounced in riotous phrenzy all the conftituted authorities in Europe;—when, not content with a liberty themfelves had eftablifhed, they wifhed to profelyte the world at large—to force their noxious draughts upon the revolting palates of lefs fantaftic patriots, and to crufade under the colours of a regenerative philofophy againft the tyrannies of the world,—they ceafed to be regarded with fpeculative indifference :—the bofoms of men began to beat with generous indignation againft the invaders of their fettled authorities, and the menacing adverfaries of their ancient laws.— They faw, in the denunciations of a powerful people, the alarming precurfors of a gathering ftorm, and trembled for the fecurity of thofe eftablifhments which cement the bonds of fociety. The flames of animofity were juftly kindled againft the infolent pretenders to univerfal empire; and the abhorrence of a nation which menaced religion, good faith, and civil authority, was not without reafon regarded as a teft of virtue, of honour, and of patriotifm.

Since

Since the commencement of thofe meafures
which have carried the Britifh arms againft this
infatuated country, the progrefs of iniquity in
their factious Reformers has become more
rapid; and the hideous mafs of their preceding crimes has been augmented by enormities
which find no parallel in the calendar of iniquity. The unexpected check which their
ambition experienced in the repulfion of their
armies from our menaced Ally—the precipitate
retreat of their debilitated forces from the
fattening foil of the conquered Netherlands—
the defection of Dumourier, and the death of
Dampiere—the fall of Valenciennes, of Mentz,
and Toulon; thefe feverally agitated the public fpirit:—each event that damped their ardor
fharpened their acrimony, and turned their
luft of conqueft into a temper of revenge.
Hence the diftractions of divided factions, and
the feverities that fell upon the weaker parties! Hence the fcaffold was feen to drink
up the blood of the innocent, and profcription
to replace the exhaufted treafures of fucceffive defeats! The caufe of enthufiafm could
alone be fupported by brilliant achievements;
and the fhock that arrefted the current of profperity, might prove fatal to the exiftence of

C 4   the

the public delufion. To divert therefore the mind from a contemplation of danger, and to remove the impreffion of impending calamity, fome barbarous expedients muft be devifed to keep the paffions alive ; and fome feats performed of general intereft. Hence the vengeance which followed each event of national defeat :—Difappointments were healed by fome bloody facrifice, and the wrongs of ill fortune were punifhed in the victims of her caprice. The public was taught to regard the arms of the Republic invincible by all but the arts of corruption :—Hence their towns are carried by *intrigue,* their armies vanquifhed by *bribery*—the conquefts of their adverfaries are faid to be made oftener by circumvention than by courage ; and all the defeats themfelves experience, are afcribed rather to the inexperience of the conquered than to the intrepidity of the conquerors. The ill-fated leaders of routed fquadrons are arraigned for crimes in which Fortune has difappointed the exertions of courage ; and atone, by their lives, for loffes which they could not prevent :—in them failure is treated as a mark of incivifm ; and a want of fuccefs regarded as a want of fidelity. The country they ferved is feen to

fallen

faften upon their declining prowefs; to fupply
the default of their accufation by fictitious
charges, and facrifice at the altar of vindictive
refentment the guiltlefs defenders of an un-
grateful authority.

But it is not their injuftice, it is not their
ingratitude, it is not their public violence that
provoke the indignation of Britifh fenfibility.
It is not that tearing up the inftitutions of antiquity, and violating the ordinances of their
own eftablifhment, they are introducing havock and anarchy into every department of
their empire ;—it is not that violating the faith of
nations, they are trampling upon all the rights
of proftrate humanity ;—it is not that profcrib-
ing the innocent and the virtuous, they are
exalting and dignifying the criminal and the
profligate;—it is not for thefe confiderations,
powerful as they may be to wound the feelings, that Englifhmen glow with generous indignation : the crimes of France are of a ftill
deeper dye, and the enormities of this nation
poffefs ftill darker fhades of guilt and profligacy. It is, that braving the thunders of
Heaven, thefe bold invaders of all that is venerable and facred in the inftitutions of the
world,

world, have fpoiled fociety of its hallowed
fanctuaries, and deftroyed the altars of Chriftian adoration : it is that rifing above the
ordinary level of facrilegious infolence they
have carried the arms of deftructive Reformation into the temples of immemorial worfhip; and not only fubverted the fhrines of
a corrupt faith, but even profcribed, with un-
recorded fcepticifm, the univerfal principle of
an acknowledged Divinity !

In our own country the public profeffion of
a religious character was, perhaps, in no period of our hiftory more generally admitted ;
and the authentic fanctions of the Chriftian
faith was in no period of reformed religion
more univerfally acknowledged. In a nation
like our own, numerous in its population, and
fublime in its public character ; great in arms
and imperious in commerce, all the vices of
civilized luxury will find their place ;—but,
viewing in an eftimate of equitable allowance,
the prominent features of the Britifh character,
it will not be found that religious influence
exifts in fo reduced a proportion as is generally imagined. That Chriftianity fails of its
due authority in controlling the fallies of fafhion-
able

able diffipation, and operating the purity of
dignified example, will readily be allowed ; and
thofe who are interefted in its univerfal domi-
nation, will fecretly deplore the obftructions to .
its empire :—yet, admitting the prevalence of
vice and corruption ; admitting the influence of
practical depravity, the fanctions of Chriftianity
ftand at leaft undifputed; whatever corruptions
may tarnifh the conduct, the fyftem of faith is
at leaft defended from facrilegious degradation;
whatever crimes or follies may deform the purity of practical character, ftill the bounds of
virtue and vice are religioufly preferved ; and
the rites of devotion are revered by thofe who
are abandoned, to the pollutions of vice and
immorality. We have not yet caught ·the con-
tagious influence of Gallic infidelity, nor become profelytes to the credulity of their blafphe-
mous fcepticifm. We hear with abhorrence the
rumour that reports their wretched philofophy :
and the violence they have offered to the fhrines
of the Deity, endear to us more tenderly the
altars of domeftic worfhip. To us the honour
of Religion is of no fmall eftimation in the
fcale of public policy. The celebration of its
rites is by us maintained with a zeal and refpect
that proclaim its influence in the fphere of
autho-

authority; all its fanctions are by us claffed among the acknowledged records of undif- puted veracity; and the obfervance of its infti- tutions is connected with the firft duties of civil obligation.

Untouched therefore by the phrenzy of political diftraction; uncontaminated by the poifon of irreligious wantonnefs;—the coun- try we boaft ftands exempt from the mala. dies of that innovating Philofophy which, in pufhing refinements to all the heights of imaginary excellence, attenuates the finews of Government, and evaporates the vigour of au- thority. While fecure amidft the carnage of obnoxious Adminiftration, our Rulers poffefs the public confidence;—while fafe from the impreffion of a foreign enthufiafm, our citizens difcover the firmnefs of undeviating loyalty, it becomes a duty of no common obligation to cherifh the exiftence of this rational una- nimity, and to protect the fobriety of the public conviction by all the arts of a faga- cious policy,—that the fhocks of violence, or the ftratagems of fubtlery, may introduce no weaknefs into the eftablifhments of the empire; and that the fabric of our Government, and the
infti-

inftitutions of our religion may be preferved inviolate amidft the tumults of foreign hoftility,
and the turbulence of domeftic difcontents.

To meliorate the ftate of defective adminiftration, to purge the channels of corrupt authority, to drag forth influence from its hidden
fortreffes, and drive from their lurking ambufh
the forces of oppreffion, are privileges dear to
the feelings of freedom; privileges facred in
the code of Britifh rights: they are interwoven
with the principles of conftitutional independ-
ence, and are commended to our regard by
the fentiments of our firft Legiflators, and the
example of our moft diftinguifhed patriots.
By thefe our anceftors have eftablifhed that
freedom which, combining the energies of
authority with the rights of humanity, attracts
the fteady attachment of enlightened patriotifm.
By thefe the privileges of a generous government muft be maintained in all the luftre of
original inftitution, and handed down to a late
pofterity untarnifhed by corruption, untorn by
licentioufnefs. There are, however, periods
in the hiftory of a nation, in which principles,
the moft unalterable, muft fuffer a temporary
fufpenfion; in which the ingenuous zeal of pa-

triotic

triotic reform muft intermit its active functions.
There are moments in which the magnitude
of the evil is diminifhed by the dangers attending its removal; moments, in which the violence of the remedy may furpafs the virulence
of the difeafe; and the continuance may be
judged lefs formidable than the cure. It has
not, without reafon, been contended by thofe
who calculate the ftate of fociety upon a fcale
of comprehenfive policy, that to fuch a period
England is now arrived; and that the unparalleled crifis of political ferment offers no fecurity for the wifdom of reforms. That falutary
correctives might with juftice be applied to the
different orders of exifting authority, is a truth
which obfervation attefts; a truth which fhould
never be ceded to fear, nor facrificed to ac-
commodation; it is a truth which exifting
abufes proclaim, and which loyalty unites with
patriotifm to imprefs indelibly upon the heart.
Tardinefs and exaction degrade our courts, and
venality and corruption difgrace our public
functionaries; laws the moft rigorous have fur-
vived their ufes, and ftatutes the moft degrading
continue uncancelled. The Reprefentation of
the country has departed from its ancient purity,
and exhibits in its ftate of modern corruption,

a ftriking

a ſtriking contraſt to its primitive inſtitution. The fact is notorious; and whatever ſophiſtry may plead in its defence, the evils which flow from its diſtorted functions are not to be meaſured by any rule of conjecture. In a country conſtituted upon the principles we acknowledge, the ſtrongeſt ſecurity for found adminiſtration exiſts in the due balance of the ſeparate orders, and the juſt proportion of that authority which the laws of the empire have annexed to each. The fureſt means of preſerving this equipoiſe is, by continuing inviolate the repreſentation, and by repelling corruption from that important body, which is conſtituted the organ of the people's wiſhes, and interpoſed as a counterbalance againſt ariſtocratic influence. The ſplendor of Ariſtocracy will ſupport its own privileges; and the throne of its authority is not found to experience much fluctuation. It is in the ſpirit of all bodies, to which ſociety has annexed ſuch flattering diſtinctions, to maintain their influence in its moſt ample extent, and to ſuffer no deduction from their weight in the ſcale of political authority. This was early ſeen in the hiſtory of this country, under a tyrannical yet puſillanimous monarch *. The

* King John.

determined jealoufy of the privileged orders
fet bounds to the widening influence of the
crown, and preferved, by the compactnefs of
their union, the fplendor of their privilege.
The memory of this event is immortalized by
the production of a *charter*, the proudeft in
the annals of the world ; and can only fall with
the falling conftitution. To the Ariftocracy
of this country we owe fome gratitude ; nor can
we withhold a due veneration to that authority
which ftruck the rock from whence gufhed the
fprings of freedom. Raifed upon thrones of
ancient dignity, furrounded by privileges of
ample extent, the Ariftocracy of the country
may be confidered as flourifhing in its proudeft
luxuriancy at the prefent day, and covering,
at leaft, as wide a fphere as is compatible with
the fpirit of the conftitution. Yet, exalted as it
ftands in the fcale of fociety, generoufly as it
is endowed by the inftitutions of the realm, it
poffeffes but the luftre of a mild fupremacy,
and wields no weapons of defiance againft the
rights of the citizen, or the equal laws of the
empire : it was modified by ancient wifdom,
and circumfcribed by corrective patriotifin ;
it is clothed with the diftinctions of unoppreffive
fplendor, and furnifhed with the inftruments
of untyrannizing influence ; it is decorated with
the

the infignia of patrimonial honours, and covered
with the fpoils of anceftral atchievements ; it is
furrounded with a blaze of ancient glory, and
glows with the luftre of recorded virtues ; its
monuments preferve the memory of our fame,
and the brighteft events of our hiftory are read
in its efcutcheons ; all the arms of violence are
wrefted from its hands, and its exertions are
coerced by inviolable laws ; its range is fixt by
impaffable limits ; its influence circumfcribed
by imperious authority ; it ftands corrected and
controlled by that invincible energy which de-
fines and protects the rights of all ; it claims no
pre-eminence in the guardianfhip of its property
above that of the humbleft freeholder ; its pof-
feffions are fubject to the fame charters, are
amenable to the fame judicature, and charge-
able (in fome few inftances excepted) to the fame
national burdens which are meafured out pro-
portionably to the capacities of all.

As a tumultuous outcry has been raifed againft
the exiftence of ariftocratic diftinctions ; as
thefe have been reprefented by the champions
of republicanifm as abhorrent from nature,
and full of oppreffion,—it may not be amifs to
enter more at large into the political utility of

fuch

fuch diftinctions, and the pofitive advantages which thefe contribute in the adminiftration of an extenfive empire. The public ears have indeed been fickened with the diffufe difcuffions of queftions which involve the theory of politics ; but in deference to thofe able and acute writers, who have inftructed the world upon fubjects of this fcience, fufficient attention appears not uniformly to have been paid to the fimpler points of practicability and expediency, upon which turns the excellence of political fyftems. Nature has been reforted to as fovereign arbitrefs of civil right ; and her dictates have been affumed as the infallible oracles of adminiftrative authority. But furely it is contradicting the fenfe of mankind, to contend that the refined policy of civilized life is to be judged by the defective laws of primitive barbarifm. To afcend through all the gradations of polifhed life, to wade backward through all the regulations of advanced fociety, to renounce the aids of an experience operated by the toil of fucceffive ages, is to lofe the privilege of a mellowed wifdom, is to facrifice the advantages of progreffive civilization, and to encounter all the unneceffary dangers of an untried expedient. There is befides, in the language of this
philofophy,

philofophy, no fmall degree of weaknefs and abfurdity. To contend that nature is paramount to all authority : What is it but to contend that the elements are fuperior to the mafs, and the foundation to the fuperftructure? This may or may not exift; and its truth, in application to civil government, will appear, not from a comparifon of refinement in general with unadulterated fimplicity, but of the different forms of civilized eftablifhment with the primitive laws of nature. Were all in nature perfect, it might with reafon be contended, that every projected improvement of nature is an act of ufurpation, and every departure from her fimplicity is but a decline towards imperfection and deformity. But no fuch perfection is found in thofe laws which Nature divulges ; and the fyftems which fhe prefcribes have neither comprehenfion nor energy fufficient to commend their application in a higher ftate of civilization. The fact is, that Nature dictates alone for that ftate in which her impulfes can be with fafety indulged; her reign is circumfcribed within that fphere and by that period in which felf-prefervation is found a principle competent to the exigencies of life, and a fufficient fecurity for the exiftence of harmony. But the mul-

tiplication

tiplication of individuals multiplies thofe paffions which would interrupt the focial agree-
ment ; and in proportion to the augmentation
fociety receives, the difficulty increafes of a
co-exiftence upon the narrow principles of natural affociation, and by the fimple expedients
of primitive inftitution. Fictions become neceffary in the advancement of fociety, to en-
courage emulation in the fphere of active life ;
to check, with reciprocal jealoufies, the turbulence of individuals ; to form juft gradations
in the fcale of authority, and give a fpring to
the political machine, by communicating an
action among its feveral parts. Without ex-
panding this reafoning into all that extent of
which it would admit, it is eafy to fee how
out of fuch exigencies, and to accomplifh fuch
purpofes, diftinctions may arife which have no
exiftence in nature; and how eftablifhments
may enter into the mafs of fociety, juftifiable
alone by the neceffity which gave them birth,
and the utility which commends their continuance. It is eafy to fee in fuch a contemplation of
the fubject, that government is, in all fhapes,
a fpecies of ufurpation ; and that all diftinctions
which compofe its inftitutions, or arife out of
its exiftence, are fo many violations of natural
fimplicity ;

fimplicity; and are as incompatible with abftract right as they are conducive to general
fecurity.

Could we afcertain with juft precifion a ftate
of nature, a ftate in which the primitive rights
of man might be fully acknowledged, without
the inconvenience of arming each member of
the community againft the other;—could we
picture to ourfelves that immaculate fociety,
who partake as the common offspring of nature, all the luxuries of her bounty, and the
equal rights of her children, it would quickly
appear how little could be inferred from fo circumfcribed a groupe, in confidering the exigencies of a numerous body; and how dif-
fimilar the circumftances of fo confined a
community from the intricate complexities of
augmented fociety:—it would readily be feen
how inadequate are the regulations which conduct the firft to the coercive difcipline in the
adminiftration of the latter; and, in fine, how
inapplicable would be reafonings drawn from
the one, to anfwer at all the circumftances of
the other.

It might appear fuperfluous to infift upon
the incongruity of *natural equality* with *poli-*

tical

tical subordination: in other circumstances than
the present, it would certainly become an use-
less enforcement of an undisputed truth :—and
it has been contended on the part of those
who brandish the weapons of revolutionary law,
that no *such equality* as would reduce mankind
to one common standard is intended in their
creed; that it forms no part of their system,
and constitutes no object in the scheme of
their reform. I would gladly repose in the
faith of such declaration ; nor would I so far
impeach the good sense of this country as to
suppose that principles so inconsistent with national freedom, principles so subversive of political authority, can be cherished by the re-
spect of any one whom the public regards with
veneration and esteem. I would not for a
moment suppose that a constitution which was
the result of exerted talents and integrity ; a
constitution which blends the happy expedients of public honour and private security ; a
constitution for which heroes have fought and
patriots bled, should so far have lost its weight
with those who are shaded by its influence as
to fall before the forms of an imaginary policy,
and yield to the pretensions of a barbarous
equalization.

What

What may indeed have fheltered behind
the thick cover of a ftubborn Patriotifm;
what may have entwined among the forward
fhoots of fpontaneous loyalty, it remains for
the readers of our future hiftory to decide;
yet, indecifive upon the queftion which regards our own, we are but too fully enlightened upon the politics of our enemies;
and however ambiguous may be the maxims
of our own reformers, no doubts can longer be
entertained upon the motives and the policy of
our neighbours. Whatever may have been contended by their ancient advocates at periods
when the novel terms of their political creed
admitted a vague and equivocal interpretation,
the circumftances of fuch ambiguity have now
been fucceeded by events of explicit interpretation, and the grounds of their defence muft
be changed, or themfelves configned to their
merited infamy. Whatever complexity might
be found in the outline of their original proceedings is now completely unravelled: their
fubfequent acts have become the cleareft comment upon their doubtful fyftems, and blazoned in bloody characters the fenfe of their
decrees. The mafk is now dropped on their part,
and the equality they publifh fpurns the veil
once affirmed of a juft and an equitable policy.

Lawlefs

Lawlefs depredation fupports the polluted
thrones of their ufurping rulers, and maffacre
and profcription are expounding the text of
their civil code. All the bridled paffions of
barbarous nature are purpofely let loofe upon
the higher orders of fociety ; the characters
of the wealthieft individuals are impeached,
and the inviolable fanctuary of property forced
to exalt into confequence the plunderers of the
nation : havock marches with giant-ftrides, and
popular phrenzy regards the carnage of furviving probity with guilty exultation. While
acts of outrage were perpetrated in tumult ;
while thefe were confined to the infolence of
a mob, though connived at and tolerated by
an inefficient judicature,—nature might revolt
at the deeds of hellifh emprize yet the crime
was incomplete, and the infamy wanted its perfection. But when the firft authority of the
land is feen to originate plans of the moft glaring iniquity ; when the Legiflative Affembly en-
rolls amongft its records decrees of public fei-
zure and flagrant confifcation ; when by laws
of its own enacting the rich are humbled to
the infolence of the poor, and honour is tranf-
ferred to the refufe of mankind; when the
virtuous defenders of a juft fubordination are
butchered upon the fcaffold, and the buft of an
assassin

affaffin ╆ repofed amidft the fhrines of the Gods;
when outrages like thefe are originated and
fanctioned by that authority which has conftituted itfelf expofitor of the law,—it can no
longer remain a doubt with the virtuous in
what eftimation their principles are to be regarded : their conduct precludes at once pal-
liation and defence ; their fyftems and their ini-
quities are ~~intervened~~ *entwined* in each other; and the
Defenders of their Policy muft be confidered as the
Apologifts of their crimes.

But to return. Admitting therefore (and no
one will venture to difpute it) that diftinctions
which exift not in nature may yet become indif-
penfable to the peace and harmony of civilized
bodies, and be warranted in their inftitution by
the fovereign law of general utility ; admitting
alfo, that fictitious limits will imperceptibly arife
out of the circumftances of fociety in its progrefs
to refinement; admitting, that in bodies, whofe
members are numerous, fuch diftinctions muft
exift in a greater or lefs degree, and that whether permanent or fluctuating, whether hereditary or perfonal, fome flattering appendages
will attach to thofe whom authority or property, public influence or private aggrandizement have exalted above the reft; allowing
thefe

thefe points, it will appear that in all bodies
coalefcing into a compact of civil fociety,
whatever be their degree of purity, the fimplicity of Nature is deftroyed; the laws of her pro-
mulging fuperfeded by thofe which neceffity
infpires; or, if continued as the elements of a
more comprehenfive legiflation, they are fo
modified by circumftances, that they appear no
longer the fame. The diflinctions therefore of
Ariftocracy are not upon thefe principles unjuft,
becaufe they contradict Nature; fince all the regulations of civil fociety would in that cafe
come under the fame character. The fimplicity of
Nature merits indeed our admiration, and is un-
doubtedly to be obferved fo far as is confiftent
with the complicate neceffities of a numerous fociety; but when Nature fhall have delivered
her oracles, they muft, after all, be tried by
the rule of utility, and fubmit to the paramount
authority of the public good.

Simplicity is indeed laid down by the ftrenuous advocates of a free government, as ef-
fential to the exiftence of general liberty; and
it has been not a little infifted upon that a
reprefentative legiflation, unfhackled by the
pre-eminence of a Monarch, or the influence
of

of an Ariſtocracy, is the only ſecurity for the
rights of mankind. The theory, as defended
by its ableſt advocates, poſſeſſes indeed no
ſmall recommendation, and appears to offer
(ſuppoſing it practicable) no inconſiderable emolument to the world at large. And were I con-
fident of individual virtue, were I ſecure of
private patriotiſm, I would readily aſſent in
the choice of a Government to the uncorrupt
ſimplicity ſo ſtrenuouſly recommended. Had I
reliance upon the integrity of individual exertions; could I repoſe in the conſtancy of public
ſpirit,—I would accede to the demands of
unreſtricted freedom ; I would aſſign to the
delegates of the people an authority paramount
to all control, and make the organs of the
public voice the ſole adminiſtrators of the public functions; I would implead as innovations
all diſtinctions that exiſted not upon general
conſent, and ſuffer all authorities to bow to
the Majeſty of the People.

But while the paſſions of mankind poſſeſs
their turbulence; while diſcord divides the
bonds of union, and violence diſtorts the
functions of reaſon ; while intereſt tramples
upon integrity, and private emolument ſwal-
lows up public virtue, I would not commit the
ſolid

folid concerns of a great empire to the mercy
or the caprice of a fluctuating body; I would
not feek a refinement to which the portion of
exifting virtue is not competent; nor would I
fuffer the veffel of ftate to float, like the ark of
old, upon the heaving bofom of tumultuous
waves, nor expofe its ftability to the tampering
experiments of fucceffive innovations.

It has been contended, that a Government
conftructed upon principles of fimplicity, poffeffes advantages, to which a complicated fyftem,
like our own, can never pretend. I am ready
to allow the juftice of the obfervation with refpect to fome particulars: I am ready to admit
that œconomy may be beft confulted, and the
evils of corruption moft fuccefsfully detected
in a fcheme of Government whofe parts are
few, and whofe adminiftrators are not dignified
by the appendages of rank and influence: but
there is a defect in all fuch fyftems, which pre-
ponderates in evil againft the combined advantages which they pretend to beftow. Whatever
be their commendations in the fphere of theory,
to the eye of experience they prefent no
charms; they want that permanence, that vigor, and that uniformity which fyftems exhibiting

biting more complicacy are found to poffefs. Nothing is more harraffing to the feelings, nothing more formidable to the fecurity of individuals, than a government whofe wheels are lightly hung, and whofe laws are expofed to the perpetual fluctuations of difcretionary policy. There is lefs evil in the fettled feverity of rigorous defpotifm, than in the capricious benignity of an unfteady freedom; and the poffible ills of repeated change prefent more horror than the defined exaction: of uniform tyranny.

In ftates, where the rude hand of oppreffion has enchained the national will, and impregnated with defpotifm all the channels of authority, the vaffal learns to know his allotted fphere, and to afcertain the limits of his circumfcribed range; he partakes, without alarm, the fcanty boon affigned him; bends, by habitude, to the circumftances of his lot, and finds in the uniformity of public protection a counterbalance to the wrongs of fervitude. But in a ftate where the movements of Government are lefs fteadily directed; where the ardor of melioration deftroys confidence in prefent decifions; and where the ordinances of the empire

are

are committed rather to the difcuffion of the
philofopher than the execution of the magiftrate,—the evils of uncertainty poffefs a baneful magnitude. There no roots can penetrate
the ftubborn foil ; no permanence confolidates
the bloffoms of freedom, nor mellows into ma-
turity the fruits of wholefome authority.

Tranfported by the flattering delufion of the
moment, the enthufiaftic patriot exults in his
imagined fuperiority ; when fuddenly the hori-
zon of his felicity is darkened ; the forces of the
reigning yield to the ftrength of the rifing faction, and the laws which were ftamped with
paft approbation are caft into the new mould
of a more perfect policy. Where, amidft fuch
clafhing factions, can private fecurity and reciprocal confidence exert their gentle radiance ?
Jealous diftruft fits brooding around, and the
fuperiority that's fought or dreaded, moves the
pang of envious difcontent.

Ambitious to exalt himfelf in the public
efteem, by more than ordinary effufions of patriotic zeal, each afpires to rife above the other
in the fcale of eftimation, rather than of virtue;
and as jealoufy or envy, as hope or fear infpire,
                                                    each

each labours to aggrandize his own fame in the
public opinion, by impeaching the purity of
rival patriotifm. Thus the harmony of focial
union is interrupted; the tranquil pleafures of
repofe are loft in the tumults of contentious ri-
valry; and the gentler laws of attachment are
profcribed by the rigorous maxims of an un-
feeling Patriotifm. Hence, in the hiftory of
ancient ftates, fuch experiments appear in all inftances to have been made without effect; and
from the accidents which were infeparable from
this feeming good, a thoufand ills of the moft
baneful malignity have been feen to flow. The
evil paffions have enjoyed an ample licence under the faireft femblance of virtuous reftriction:
amidft the enthufiafm of an imagined liberty
have been felt the horrors of tenfold flavery:
and all the maladies of an unfound authority
have raged amidft the delufive blaze of ideal
perfection.

It has been before remarked, that one of the
ftrongeft arguments in favour of fimplicity in
the forms of Government, is the facility which
it offers in the detection of its evils, and confequently of remedying them with promptitude
and effect.

There

There is, indeed, no doubt that complicacy
and difficulty are pretty nearly connected, and
that the exifting defect in a complicate fyftem
may find fome fhelter amongft the multiplicity
of its parts. Allowing, however, that in a
Government like our own, the complicacy of
its ftructure baffles, in many particulars, the
detection of its evils; and confequently prevents
the poffibility of cure,—it muft at the fame time
be obferved, that this principle fo depreciated
gives to the conftitution a compactnefs and fo-
lidity which fewer parts and lefs dependency
among them could not produce. To the exiftence of this complicacy we owe that tempered
equipoife which the reciprocal action of the
component orders effects in their feveral functions and departments: to this complicacy we
are indebted for that permanence which the
conftitution exhibits amidft all the viciffitudes
of Europe; that ftubborn firmnefs by which
it defies the attacks of innovation, and outlives
the tumult of change: to this complicacy we
owe the energy with which it refifts the fhafts
of popular violence, and evades the noftrums
of political quackery: to this, in fhort, we owe
that rigor which it poffeffes in curbing the ob-
liquities of licentioufnefs, while it encourages
the

the glow of freedom; that invincible ftability
with which it meets the rage of party, and rifes
invulnerable from the ftorms of faction: com-
pacted by bonds of natural connection, and
fupplied with motives for emulous contention,
the orders thus at once unite and repel, coun-
teract and coalefce; their feparate advantage
dictates the firft, their common intereft urges
the laft; their jealoufies involve no difcord,
their harmony no intrigue; and their union and
their counteraction equally ferve the preferva-
tion of all.

It might further be remarked, that the facility of detecting the unfoundnefs of the parts,
efteemed among the moft advantageous characteriftics of fimple forms of Government, may
not upon all principles be deemed a good. No
evil in a ftate can rife, in point of baneful magnitude, above the turbulent mifchiefs of continual reform. The perpetual application of
remedial policy to the tranfient irregularities of
the governing fyftem, leads to debilities as in-
jurious and enervating to the body politic as
the continual tampering with medicinal potions
does to the natural conftitution. In all ftates
of civil fociety evil will blend with good, and

vice will adulterate the purity of virtue: while humanity retains its wonted characteriftics, corruption will grow out of the noxious flock of human depravity; and in the ample fphere of an extended adminiftration the luxuriant fhoots of private intereft will entwine among the vigorous branches of public principle. It were vain to expect in the imperfect reign of political virtue, an authority purged of all oppreffion, a patriotifm devoid of all felf-intereft: it were vain to expect that the orders of ftate fhould drop the paffions of humanity, and that public bodies fhould ftand exempt from that bias which individuals obey.

Simplicity therefore, in the ftructure of a Government, is expofed to objections of ferious magnitude; and, in obviating the mifchiefs of an intricate fyftem, gives birth to diforders of more frequent recurrency, and more fatal extent than thofe which it affects to remove. While it expofes to ready detection the nafcent evil, it keeps the public fpirit in a temper of fluctuating uncertainty; while it checks the infinuations of gradual corruption, it keeps alive the rankling difcontents of a jealous patriotifm; while it curbs the growth of fubtle tyranny, it retards

the

the advancement of fteady authority; opens, by a thoufand diffentions, the clofing wounds of faction, and adminifters eternal fuel to the flames of difcord.

Hitherto we have proceeded upon the abftract queftion of Theoretic Politics, and have all along fuppofed a Government to be formed. This, however, is not the fituation in which we ftand: the queftion, as it regards ourfelves, is not Whether we fhall eftablifh a fyftem of Monarchy or Republicanifm? but, Whether we fhall exchange the latter for the former? Whether we fhall fubvert the one, in order to eftablifh the other?

Suppofing therefore, that the arguments in behalf of Republicanifm were deemed valid in the fcale of reafoning againft thofe which fupport the claims of Monarchy; fuppofing, that in the comparifon of difputed forms the fcale had preponderated in favour of reprefentative authority; the argument muft take a new turn when applied to the demolition of an exifting Government; and the reafoning which demonftrated in the cafe of election, would not have been conclufive in the cafe of exchange.

E 2   Pre-

Prejudice is the inevitable offspring of habit, and, under some shape and in a certain degree, exercises its influence over minds of every description. Prejudices imbibed in early infancy; prejudices tranfmitted by fucceffive generations, and rendered dear by fuppofed advantages connected with them, shoot deep their roots into the foil of affection, and are not eafily torn from the tenacious bofom. It is true that in proportion as the underftanding acquires its vigor, and the mind perfects its information, this habitual bias diminifhes its influence; and the mind, enlarged by comprehenfive fcience, becomes more competent to equitable decifion. Yet, even amidft the blaze of matured knowledge, and in the zenith of advanced refinement, prejudices fuffer not a total extirpation: fome late remains ftill cling around the heart, and chain the affection of mankind to forms under which they once have flourifhed, and eftablifhments from which they once derived protection and fecurity. Whatever therefore may be the recommendations of a new fyftem; however fpecious may be its advantages; however it may rife in wifdom and in luftre above the diminifhed attractions of the old, yet there are inconveniencies attending the exchange,

exchange, which nothing fhould induce mankind to encounter but corruption the moft
enormous, infolence the moft oppreffive, and
mifery the moft profound. An hoft of inveterate
prejudices arm againft thofe reforms which would
tear down the monuments of ancient wifdom,
brand with ignominy all the inftitutions of ancient policy, and demolifh the idolized forms
of immemorial ufage. Some refpect is in all
cafes to be paid to thofe attachments which a
feries of ages has begotten, and which a long
familiarity has confolidated; which have grown
out of early fenfibilities, and kept pace with
the vigor of progreffive paffion: thefe may be
purged by reafon, and mollified by reflection;
they may be filenced by prudence, they may
be fuppreffed by fear; yet, in moments of oc-
cafion, their embers will glow, and their vigor
revive: rebellious againft thofe authorities
which have combated their influence, they
will embarrafs the progrefs of novel inftitutions,
and fhow, by obftacles of ferious diftraction,
that though variable in their energy, they are
indeftructible in their effence; and though di-
vifible from the judgment, they are infeparable
from the heart.

At-

Attached by long and felicitous experience
to a monarchical fyftem, the breaft of an Eng-
lifhman harbours ten thoufand prejudices in
favor of that authority from which he fup-
pofes himfelf to have derived fuch fplendid
advantages; he looks back upon the æras of
change recorded in the annals of his country,
and finds fome of the nobleft ftruggles of patriotic virtue exercifed in fupport of that authority which he is proud to cherifh; he calls
up to view the luminous events which circumfcribed the Monarch's throne, without facrificing the luftre of prerogative, and expanded
the rights of freedom without pouring in the
flood of licentioufnefs; he glances with horror
over that period which gave up the nation to
the havock of Republicanifm; over that period
in which a fyftem of unexampled oppreffion
was eftablifhed by the pretended Reformers of
an abufed authority, and the boafting adhe-
rents of a meliorating policy. Would he filence
the advocates of modern reform, he points to
that epoch of tumult and regicide when the
national fury was let loofe upon the orders of
ftate, and all was given up to confufion and to
change: he bids them eye the dread diforders
which followed thefe events, and covered with

cala-

calamity the face of the realm. The bonds of ancient compact are diffolved, the forces of difcontent are exalted, and the glory of England is committed to the ravages of a faction :—property, talents, and equity, do homage to poverty, ignorance, and injuftice :—the extravagance of a Monarch is replaced by the infolence of a demagogue ; the ambition of priefts fuccceded by the enthufiafm of fanatics, and the defpotifm of one exchanged for the tyranny of many. He fixes with attention upon the fhouts which hailed departed faction, and the triumphs that purfued recovered Monarchy: he dwells with rapture upon thofe efforts of Patriotifm which again defined the bounds of authority, and gave, in the event of a great Revolution †, an example at once to the oppreffor and the oppreffed : he traces, in the actors of this dignified fcene, principles that echo to the feelings of his heart : he regards their labours as teeming with wifdom, and abounding in intereft : he eyes the caution which accompanied their enterprizes, and the prudence which tempered their refolves : he views them emulous of their country's honour, and ftudious to fupport the

† 1683.

lan-

languid ftate; holding together the divided
chain, and fupplying with promptnefs the pernicious chafm : he obferves them reftoring rather than precipitating the tottering fabric, and
confolidating by a new force the debilitated authority : he perceives amidft the diftractions
of revolutionary tumult no fpirit of factious
riot; no rage of confifcation and plunder : he
reads no tales of flaughtered innocence : he
hears no clamours of *equalizing* outrage : he
views the vacant throne furrounded by the conciliated bands of difunited parties; the wheels
of ftate conducted by a fictitious inftrument
of fubftituted authority; till the diadem was
placed upon a more deferving head, and
Government was reftored to its accuftomed
energy.

If it be ftill contended that fuch reafoning
participates too ftrongly of prejudice, and that
the bias of opinion contributes more to its
prevalence than the ftrength of reafon,—it muft
be replied, that there are prejudices which the
wife would not difown, nor the rational dif-
claim : prejudices which expediency prompts
us to cherifh; and which prudence forbids us
to renounce. Circumftances might be affigned
in

in human life which prefent formidable dangers to naked contemplation; and fcenes in which the mind, ftripped of its native prejudices, encounters a ferious rifque. Nor is this all; fome deference is furely due to the uninfluenced decifions of enlightened minds: fome delicacy is furely to be exercifed in judging the public labours of experienced Legiflators: fome caution fhould be employed in criticifing the talents and the patriotifm of thofe who fpurned the tamenefs of abject fubmiffion, and caft the forms of eftablifhed authority in the mould of generous freedom. Armed with the forces of revolutionary law, they precipitated the Monarch, yet preferved the monarchy; they banifhed the tyrant, yet guarded inviolable the rights of the throne. Yet they were not in a ftate of ignorance as to the different advantages of the varied modes of Government; nor were they (as fome would pretend) left afloat amidft the waves of political fcepticifm. They could advert to paft experience; they could borrow wifdom from the conduct of preceding Legiflators. The evils of Monarchy were felt by them in all their painful extent; yet Monarchy continued to preferve their attachment, and determine their choice. They

were

were not ignorant of the claim which Republicanifm might poffefs, to a preference in the
conftitution of a Government :—The ex eri-
ment had in their hiftory been tr d ; and its
pretenfions afcertained to their fulleft exten : all
its advantages muft have been prefent to their
view ; all its recommendations ftrong in their
recollection: they could judge with compe-
tency how far it was fuited to the genius of
the people, and the condition of the empire.
In addition to thefe confiderations, they had
incitements to Republicanifm, which neither
the factious in France nor the difcontented in
Britain could at this day pretend to exhibit.
Oaths and covenants the moft facred had been
violated by the * Royal Prevaricator ; acts of
outrage and of tyranny had been perpetrated
by him in defiance of law, and in contempt of
remonftrance ; fear had prompted him to precipitate flight, and the country was now delivered from a deliberate tyranny. If ever
therefore Monarchy might be deemed inex-
pedient, it would furely be moft reafonably fo
at a crifis when the enormities of the Sovereign
were read in the tumult of the country : if

* James II.

ever

ever Republicanifm might command a preference, it furely would moft naturally have
triumphed in that moment when the public
refentment glowed againft the fugitive Monarch, and the diforganized authorities were
in a fituation to admit political experiment.
Except therefore we maintain the prefump-
tuous claims to a light which never gleamed
upon preceding patriots; except we cherifh the
boaftful delufion of a knowledge which efcaped
the fages who have taught us, we muft yield
fome deference to thofe who compaffed the Revolution upon which we repofe : we muft allow
fome degree of weight to their decifions; who,
amidft the blaze of triumphant Patriotifm, immortalized their attachment to limited monarchy.

Admitting therefore, that ancient prejudices
influence, to no fmall extent, the patriotic
fpirit of the prefent times; and that habitual
bias acts powerful in rivetting our attachment
to monarchy, we have at leaft the fatisfaction
of treading in the fteps of no mean Patriots; we
have at leaft the confolation of fupporting an
authority which found fupporters in the proudeft
luminaries of Britifh hiftory. It is true, the
Pa-

Patriots of a century paft had not the advantages of thofe fuperior difcoveries which make fo prominent a figure in the fphere of modern politics: Prieftly had not dealt 1 ‘ republican menaces; Paine had not uttered his equalizing oracles. The defects of accident had not been magnified into irremediable diforders; the imperfections of humanity had not provoked the violence of tumultuous affault; nor had the fcattered fpirits of difaffection ranged their forces againft the depreciated inftitutions of antiquity. It was not then acknowledged in the fcience of politics, that revolutionary law is the firft principle of rational government; or that the privilege of change was the proudeft advantage of a free people: yet Milton had darted the full glare of his republican fcepticifm; yet Sydney had probed the authority of Kings; and Locke had proclaimed the duties of refiftance. Proud therefore of acting up to the wifdom of fuch anceftors, we are little emulous of outftripping their atchievements; we readily own the influence their decifions poffefs; and copy, without blufhing, the dignity of their example.

That

That the conftitution of which we boaft, and the conftitution we experience, pofiefs not an accurate refemblance to each other we are ready to allow : that in the multifarious movements of an entire century the complicate wheels of this political machine have incurred fome embarraffment, is a truth to which every reafonable man muft fubfcribe; a truth which men, higheft in the confidence of Government and the efteem of the public, have decidedly avowed; a truth which the moft outrageous advocates of the exifting Government would not prefume to controvert. But he deferves little of his injured country who, in a moment when revolutionary enthufiafm threatens to fubvert all the valuable diftinctions of civil fociety, would drag to invidious light her latent weakneffes, and inflame, by aggravated pictures of exifting grievances, the kindling rebellion of her difaffected members. It cannot, it ought not to be denied, that the influence of the Crown has paffed the conftitutional limit; that the forces of Ariftocracy have exceeded their juft proportion; that the reprefentation has, in many particulars, to venality and corruption; and that the national burthens have, by ruinous wars and languinary policy, minifter'd to the public

public felicity, and added to the mafs of inevitable mifery; but in a moment like the prefent, a moment diftinguifhed by an unparalleled ferment of the public mind; a moment when the colours of anarchy are floating in the air, and hoftilities are maintained againft all the promifcuous eftablifhments of authority and fubordination, the eye of faithful Patriotifm will glance with gentle partiality over the defects which cloud, and rather fix upon thofe excellencies which adorn the Government it wifhes to preferve; it will calculate the privileges of that authority which modern innovators affail, and teftify its fidelity to the eftablifhments themfelves, by referving the remonftrance againft their defects to periods of lefs agitation, and moments of lefs danger.

Was it ever known, was it ever recorded, that a government planned with the wifeft policy, a government conducted by the moft unimpeached fagacity, kept its juft line of uniform virtue; preferved unalterable its characteriftic excellence; repelled in every inftance the affaults of corruption, and triumphed completely over the defects of accident? The faireft example which the world produces, is
that

that government fo often infifted upon, the Republic of America ; and were the hiftory of this
country complete; had it counted up a due
feries of mellowing ages, it would ftand as an
ample refutation of all the reafonings offered
in fupport of a monarchy. But formed by the
imperious dictates of neceffity, produced from
a combination of peculiar circumftances, America will ftand for no example in deciding upon
the policy of this country : ten thoufand particulars, which cannot here be adverted to, gave
naturally rife to the fyftem of government
which regulates that empire. Separated from the
feat of ancient Sovereignty by a wide ocean,
and ftill wider animofities, it were not to be
expected that a fyftem of authority which had
excited their wars, drenched their fields, and
arrefted their commerce, would ever be adopted
by a people whom circumftances had left to
the election of their government. How far the
fyftem which now flourifhes in fuch enviable
profperity, fhall maintain its exiftence in the
ftorms which future events may excite againft
this in common with other nations, it will remain for time and pofterity to decide : it is
our part to judge of paft tranfactions alone,
and to derive our maxims of practical policy
from

from thofe experiments, which having been inftituted in paft ages, have feen all the changes
of human event, and undergone all the viciffitudes which were necefſary to the perfection
of their character.

But the paſſions of men are now heated to an
extraordinary degree; a popular phrenzy reigns
among all the lower orders of fociety, and the
ruling principle of modern philofophy is the deftruction of exifting authorities; the falchion
of reformation is brandifhed in bold defiance,
and threatens to humble, in levelled indif-
tinction, all the diverfified inftitutions of fociety.
The queftion no longer is, Whether the government we boaft have any defects? but, Whether it poffefs any virtues? The contention
no longer is, Whether it deferve encomium?
but, Whether it be worth preferving? A thoufand circumftances confpire to fhew, that the
prefent moment is lefs favourable to rational
reform than any which hiftory records: the
events which are tranfacting, and the doctrines
which are publifhed at the prefent crifis, are
not of that character which the patient ope-
ration of corrective policy demands. The bu-
finefs of reform is cool and deliberate; the

                                    conduct

conduct of revolution is rapid and enthufiaftic;
the one muft be tranfacted in moments of
tranquillity, the other muft be operated in the
bofom of confufion; to the one is requifite a
prudent policy, the other demands an enter-
prizing fyftem; the one reforts to experience,
the other indulges in theory; the former is
marked by cautious gradation, the latter is characterized by vigorous precipitance. It would
be fuperfluous to infift upon the ftrict appli-
cability which the formidable characteriftics
of the latter poffefs, to the fermenting intem-
perance of modern politics : if therefore the
correction of abufes, if the remediation of defects be the innocent objects of clamorous patriotifm; if behind the colours of reform no
harpies of equalization fhelter their deftructive
venom ; if thofe who demand the purification
wifh not the fubverfion of the conftitution, then
let them intermit thofe ill-timed remonftrances
which affift the murmurs of fedition, and fhake
the attachment of unfettled virtue; let the mi-
nute defects of a government, impregnated with
wifdom and furrounded with benignity, be
generoufly covered to the eye of inquifitive difcontent ; let the lighter wounds of the conftitution be kept unprobed till the cutting blaft

F   of

of revolutionary phrenzy has dropped its fury, and the hemisphere of politics has recovered its serenity : then, under the aufpices of reftored tranquillity, the public mind will have recovered that fteady vigor, that collected energy, which may enable it to reform the defects without facrificing the excellencies of the conftitution, and to remedy its debilitated functions without amputating its moft valuable eftablifhments.

But all is not yet loft ; amidft the clamours of calumnious fallehood, the voice of truth has not been drowned ; her accents have prevailed above the rage of conflicting fentiments, and Europe has witneffed the fidelity of Britain. Fired with enthufiafm at the events which broke the fhackles of Gallic fervitude, we participated indeed the triumphs of a people rifing in the fcale of dignity ; a people who fhowed themfelves deferving of an exalted freedom by uniting the claims of loyalty and patriotifm. But falfe to honour, to loyalty, to patriotifm, the country once marked for the afylum of peaceful arts; the country once dear to the feelings of the patriot bofom, now wakes the refentment of indignant virtue, and draws tears of blood from the eye of degraded freedom.

Did

Did the early applaufe of Gallic emancipation need apology, it would be eafy to difcover how naturally fuch impreffions might be made upon the Britifh fenfibilities, alive to all the tranfports of generous policy. The eyes of Europe fixed with aftonifhment upon that transformed people, who from a ftate of immemorial fervitude emerged into inftantaneous liberty; the irritating enormities which fowed the feeds of this fplendid event, and the brilliant atchievements by which it was effected, made too confiderable a figure in the theatre of politics not to be confidered of momentous importance. While courts and cabinets regarded this example with political alarm, and trembled for its influence upon their vaffal fubjects, the latter eyed it as an aufpi- cious check upon the tyrannies of Europe, and hailed it as the happy prefage of their falling chains.

In Britain, where liberal authority exerts its empire; where the rights of man are blazoned in charters and acknowledged in juries,—the energies of a people afpiring at freedom could not be regarded with indifference. France had for ages diftinguifhed herfelf as the rival of the Britifh power, and the wanton difturber of

F 2   the

the Britiſh tranquillity. The memory of un-
provoked and expenſive wars, awakened by the
preſſure of every additional burden, kept alive
an animoſity of no mean degree againſt that
proud authority which had laboured by exciting
the diſſentions of ſtates to balance the fates of
Europe : an authority whoſe intrigues had em-
broiled in repeated hrſtilities nations allied
by blood and intereſt; an authority whoſe
councils had widened the wounds of diſaffection,
fanned the ſparks of diſcontent, and thwarted
the means of reconciliation.

The Britiſh nation could not view without
a ſentiment of triumph the ſubverſion of that
court, to which it owed the loſs of ſo much
blood and the accumulation of ſo much debt :
it ſeemed but a juſt retaliation of political vengeance, that a court which had ſupported a co-
lonial revolt againſt the conſtituted authorities
of a rival nation, ſhould fall an involuntary
victim to the ſame principles, and ſuffer a
defeat upon its own territories. The events
which compoſed this diſtinguiſhed revolution
were not indeed characterized by perfect juſtice ;
but the atrocious guilt of the vanquiſhed authorities had poſſeſſed too ſtrongly the public
abhor-

abhorrence to be cancelled by events of accidental violence, or obliterated by acts of transient injustice. The councils which issued from the Court of France were distinguished by the features of interest and intrigue; and the spirit which impregnated its political measures partook alike of duplicity and oppression. Determined despot in its own sphere, it sought alliance with the legions of * distant revolt; it cherished abroad those systems which it stifled at home, and fostered a freedom in a foreign soil which it never suffered to germ within its own domains.

The sentiment therefore which naturally resulted from the bloodless triumphs over this defeated court, partook equally of generous exultation and revengeful joy; the splendor of the acts by which it was subverted, no less than the humiliating debasement of an ancient rival, commended to the rapture of British sensibility a revolution which promised such advantages to their future repose. Britain, rejoiced with the invidious enthusiasm of ancient Rome over fallen Carthage, considered the depression of its enemy

* America.

as the inevitable ground-work of its own pre-eminence, and anticipated in the regulations of a purified authority the golden age of undisturbed empire.

The joy which attended these distinguished atchievements exhibited a victory over national prejudice, which stamped no common honour upon the British character. The conduct of France had, in all ages, set at variance two people divided from each other by such narrow limits:—this prejudice thus excited, was blended with the elements of early instruction, and deemed essential to the purity of patriotism; the passions were heated by recorded facts, and inflamed by insinuated fears till an unconquerable aversion was established to that people whose perfidy we were taught to dread, and whose councils we had learned to despise. The great actors in every political game escape their due share of public infamy by the sacred protection of cabinet secresy, or the inviolability of exalted rank;—that odium therefore which should pursue the guilty authors, was in this, as in other instances, transferred to the innocent instruments; and our aversion to the councils fastened upon the executors of those

measures

meafures which interrupted the progrefs of our
peaceful arts, and turned the current of public
activity from commerce to war.

The prejudice thus generated had received
no little confirmation from the diffimilarity of
political temperament in the hiftoric character
of the two nations. While every page of Eng-
lifh record exhibits fome combat in defence
of freedom, fome reclamation againft abufe,
fome indignation at tyrannic infolence, — the
hiftory of France exhibited on the contrary a
long feries of defpotic conquefts, acquired over
the bending fervility of a paffive multitude. We
fought in vain for Sydneys and Hampdens in
the annals of France;—for charters extorted
by virtuous oppofition, and defpotifm modified
by intrepid patriotifm. No ray of dignified freedom was feen to pierce the fettled clouds of
immemorial tyranny : — the alarm never appeared to have gone forth, till the fpoils of
oppreffion had precluded the poffibility of refiftance ; and the evil was become of too ferious
a magnitude to admit of a cure. Seldom did a
murmur efcape this abject people till ruinous
war had depopulated their ftreets, and ghaftly
famine had defolated their abodes. So uniform
a compliance had marked their character, fo
continued a fervility had impregnated their con-

F 4   duct,

duct, that difgufted with the paft, we augured ill of the future; nor deemed it poffible that a people fhould emerge from flavery who had difcovered fo little the energies of freedom.

Yet the æra which fixed the dawn of Gallic freedom, fixed the downfal of Britifh prejudice. Faithful to the principles of our forefathers, we applauded that courage which broke the bonds of ancient tyranny, and triumphed in the extenfion of that liberal policy which gave to a nation, abandoned in all its epochs to proftrate fervility, all the generous privileges of an exalted freedom,

The enthufiafm, though widely, was not indeed univerfally felt. Diverfity of fyftem and different degrees of fenfibility prevented the uniformity of public opinion; and murmurs of diffatisfaction were heard to blend among the fhouts of acclamation.

It would be violating truth, it would be facrificing juftice, to applaud the individual parts of this tumultuous tranfaction, and to cover with admiration all the fpecific decrees of thefe diftinguifhed reformers. Tyranny had filled up
the

the ample meafures of its guilt; and over-
ftrained oppreffion had communicated an un-
known energy to this irritated people. The
blow was ftruck in that felicitous moment
which concurring circumftances united to de-
fign; and all the indifcretions of enthufiafm
were infufed into the hafty fyftems of an im-
petuous patriotifm. It was eafy to imagine
that amidft the havoc of univerfal reform diforders would find their place; and that acts of violence would inevitably accompany the neceffary
modification of ancient eftablifhments: but
turning an eye upon the yet blacker catalogue
of courtly crimes, perpetrated under the guilty
protection of ancient authority, the advocates
of this new fyftem found little difficulty in par-
doning the temporary injuftice of an unfettled
Legiflation; they carried their views forward
to the future moments of abated enthufiafm:
they anticipated the arrival of a more tranquil-
lized period; when a liberal policy fhould cor-
rect the errors of elementary legiflation, repair
the wounds of lacerated authorities, and remedy
the wrongs of expatriated exiles.

But vanifhed are all thofe delufory hopes;
and not Imagination's felf can conjure up a
fhade

fhade of future expectation. Foreign war and
internal faction have torn afunder the uniting
fpirits, have drawn out the deformities of national corruption, and given up to anarchy and
irreligion this promifing empire. The growing
influence of a republican affociation, whofe
forces had been encreafing during the reign of
the firft legiflature, acquired at length a fatal
augmentation; and rifing in the fcale of divided authority, bore down all thofe inftitutions which compofe the fplendid character of
the firft Revolution. All the milder lights of
equitable patriotifm were fwallowed up in the
blaze of this formidable faction *. Before the legions of fanguinary revolt were feen to fall, the
debilitated forces of a difcredited Monarchy,
and with them fell all the furviving diftinctions
of loyalty, humanity, and religion. From the
bloody epoch which fealed their guilt and fettled their authority, the terrors of the poignard have triumphed over all the confiderations
of honour and fidelity; and partly from fear,
partly from corruption, each citizen has become
the affaffin of his neighbour. The digreffion
which this people has difplayed from all the
principles of political virtue, was indeed rapid
in the order of time, yet gradual in the chain
of

* The Jacobins.

of events. Injuftice was feen to tarnifh the
fteady luftre of thofe atchievements which the
firft exertions of patriotic enthufiafm enrolled
amongft its nobleft acts; relaxed authority
gave fcope to the viler paffions, and injuftice
was fucceeded by a thoufand fiends of more fell
execution : public faith once violated, blood
and plunder became familiar objects ,of fteady
contemplation : the refinements of virtue were
no longer owned; the fenfibilities of humanity
no longer felt; injuftice faw no obftacle; profcription acknowledged no bounds :—the reformers of tyranny became the peculators of
their country, and the foil of freedom was mellowed with the blood of the innocent.

Much might be pardoned by a nation like
our own, whofe generous policy aims at no
conquefts; allows no tyranny :—much might
be indulged to enthufiaftic indifcretion by a
people whofe ftruggles for freedom have not
in all cafes kept within the channel of loyalty
and mercy ; — a people whofe vigorous patriotifm has itfelf, on fome occafions, broke
down the fences of ancient law, and fnatched
the fceptre from hereditary Sovereignty : but
infatiable revenge and unprincipled outrage
have

have turned the fcale; the feelings of fympathy can find no intereft in murderous licence, and guilt has cancelled every exifting claim to mercy and indulgence. Equally awake to loyalty and to freedom, the Britifh nation fpurns with honeft indignation the outrageous doctrines of an equalizing policy. Dear to Britons are thofe fictitious bounds which mark the gradations of civil life, and preferve the balance of eftablifhed orders. To them Monarchy affumes no terrors, Ariftocracy no oppreffion, and Subordination no fervility: with them authority is mild, and obedience rational: with them law acknowledges no diftinction, and juftice admits no exceptions: with them the crimes of the great are meafured by the fame rule of rigor which fixes the criminality of the mean; and the wrongs of the domeftic are expiated by the blood of the * noble. Jealous therefore of thofe authorities which protect their rights and guarantee their labours, Britons regard with fteady veneration that conftitution which fantaftic reformers are anxious to depreciate; this they cherifh as their deareft birth-

* Cafe of Earl Ferrers, executed for the murder of his fteward.

right,

right, and leave to minds poffeffed by rebellious intoxication, to digeft thofe purer fyftems
which would diforganize all exifting eftablifhments, and deftroy the univerfal fanctions of
civil authority.

Perhaps no crifis ever exhibited a more equal
experiment upon the temper of a nation, than
that which has lately exercifed the political
feelings of the Britifh public. Amidft the firft
effufions of Gallic enthufiafin, the energy of
Government appeared to flumber : it was juft
that a nation, whofe proudeft boaft was freedom, fhould be fuffered to fpeak the language
of conviction, and applaud or condemn the
tranfactions of Europe, without the interfering
dictates of an inquifitorial court. The multifarious difcuffion which filled up this interval,
excited no fmall commotion in the public fentiment, and the enthufiafin of the people was
not a little captivated by the flattering pretenfions of univerfal freedom. The ferment which
thus agitated all ranks of fociety, afforded an
ample fcope to thofe difcontented factions,
and thofe turbulent individuals which haunt
the lurking receffes of the pureft governments.
Among the firft were found thofe growing bo-

dies

dies whom the common principle of imagined oppreffion cements into a union of de-
cided animofity againft that authority under
which they pretend to fuffer. Among the latter
were found thofe formidable adventurers who
chalk out no line of fteady conduct for their
public labours, but, prompt to take advantage of occafions, commit the full ftock of their
talents and their credit to the doubtful hazard
of experimental policy. To thefe were added
the unprincipled and the licentious: all thofe
whofe intereft is found in the tumults of confufion, and whofe profits arife from the diforders of change. Thefe naturally ranked amongft
the admirers of fubverted authority, and blended
their licentious fhouts with the acclamations of
virtuous freedom. Had France maintained a
purer character, and confirmed by fubfequent
refinements the fanguine profpects of her firft advocates; had fhe continued her homage † to
the *Reftorer of her Liberty*, and guarded his
throne from violence and regicide; had fhe
preferved from injury the framers of her laws,
and the guardians of her religion; had fhe

† Louis XVI. was fo ftiled, after his acceptance of the
firft conftitution.

pro-

protected her citizens from plunder, and her
temples from facrilege: in a word, had fhe
fupported the fplendor of her firft decrees, and
maintained the fpirit of her primitive laws; had
fhe realized the vifions of pacific empire, and
filled up the grand outline of defenfive policy,
admiration might ftill have followed the blaze
of her fucceffive acts, and the dangers have
accrued to the Britifh empire from the enthufiafm of her admirers, or the councils of her
advocates. But apoftate from the principles herfelf had divulged; from principles to which
fhe had pledged herfelf by compacts the moft facred, by oaths the moft inviolable, France now
affumes a new character in the eye of Europe;
and juftly divorced from the affection of the
honeft and the virtuous, can retain no advocates, but among the wicked and the factious.
Thofe who adored with proftrate veneration the
early tranfactions of her firft Legiflators, have
forwardly renounced their defeated expectations,
and buried their affection for this abandoned
nation in the tombs that enclofe the mangled
limbs of her martyred patriots. They have feen
with horror the deftructive poignard planted in
the bofom of the moft virtuous citizens: they
have beheld with indignant fympathy the firft

re-

reformers of tyrannic authority blended in the havoc of a promifcuous maffacre, or furrendered to the murderous fcaffold under the infolent mockery of a pretended fentence.

Over their tombs fhall hover the gliding forms of departed virtue ; and the urn that en-clofes their relics be bathed with the tears of dejected freedom : the memory of their patri-otifm fhall be embalmed by the grateful in-cenfe of the Poet's mufe, and future ages fhall read with faithlefs wonder of their elevation and their fall.

The public fentiment has therefore been put to the faireft trial, and the refult is moft ho-nourable to the fidelity and the wifdom of a powerful nation. The flagrant direliction of honour and virtue in the conduct of our ene-mies, has taught us to renounce the enthufiafm with which we eyed their freedom, and the con-fidence we repofe in their policy. The pre-judices which fell with the falling chains of ancient tyranny, have now revived with the reviving fpirit of foreign conqueft ; their fra-ternizing vows have excited our abhorrence ; and their infolent ftrides for univerfal empire

have

have ftamped them the Depredators of human fociety. Such have been the feelings of the Britifh public; and generous refentment has penetrated the nation.

Individuals and corporations have difputed the palm of prompt obedience, and fworn to oppofe with united influence the deftruction of civil authority: the rankling animofities of private diffent have fought, in the intermiffion of their divifions, to eftablifh that calm which the common danger demands, and converted their arms of reciprocal contention into the inftruments of mutual defence. The commonwealth, emerged from the waves that threatened her exiftence, now rides in triumphant fecurity, and looks back with horror upon the tremendous gulphs which had opened for her deftruction: fhe exults in the tried fidelity of her fons, and acquires force from the impotent machinations of her defeated antagonifts.

The cup of Gallic iniquity appears now to be full; and invention cannot create a picture of increafed enormity. Dread infatuation feems to have agitated the diftempered minds of this proftitute people, and urged them to all the va-

rieties

rieties of anarchy, murder, and facrilege. While therefore the tremendous judgments of Heaven are overfpreading fo large a portion of Europe, let the inhabitants of the world learn righteoufnefs. Events have fo far feen their completion, that mankind may now calculate the balance of the whole, and deduce from the ftupendous acts of this mighty drama, the moft important leffons in religion and civil government.

The mercilefs facrifice of a guiltlefs Monarch may provoke our refentment againft the perpetrators of fo foul a deed; but when Nature has paid the tribute of forrow, reflection muft pafs to other fources, in order that an event of fuch publicity, a crime of fuch aggravated enormity, may anfwer the ends of public inftruction. We are not to regard the fuffering Monarch as a victim offered up at the fhrine of inhumanity, nor confider the effufion of his blood as the temerarious outrage of popular tumult. In him we are to behold clemency fuffering for the wrongs of tyranny; and the innocent expiating the crimes of the guilty. In the angry populace which demanded this facrifice, we are to view the formidable terrors of a people awakened from the torpor of fervitude

vitude to the phrenzy of revolutionary vengeance. We may read in the ferocity of their proceedings, a melancholy hiftory of that infenfibility which defpotifm generates in the outraged fubject, and learn the influence that tyranny poffeffes in corrupting the native propenfities of the heart. In the ruthlefs profcription of the degraded orders, the eye muft turn from the cruel fufferings of unoffending individuals, to confider thofe comprehenfive principles upon which depend the mighty movements of united millions. Extended in their number and privileges in their prerogatives beyond the bounds of even temperate injuftice, thefe orders had acquired a terrible majefty, and wantoned in the liberal exercife of unchaftifed oppreffion. The fcale once turned, no bounds could circumfcribe the burfting flames of public indignation fwelled with the memory of paft enormities, and heated by the embers of unburied infults. In the frantic triumphs which marked the demolition of their once venerated orders, retaliated vengeance is confpicuoufly read, and civil rights are feen in their turn to humble thofe privileges which once fwallowed up all civil rights.

In

In the rage that faftens upon the inftitutions of religion, and the zeal that difieminates infidelity and atheifm, are difcovered the remote effects of that ancient policy which fubjugated the confciences of men to the tyranny of priefts, and excluded the bulk of mankind from the ftudy of their religious faith. Taught to regard their eftablifhed confeffors as the fole depofitaries of the Chriftian oracles, they, at length, penetrated the fhallow deceit, and with a confequence drawn from their authorized fyftems, have madly deemed, that in abolifhing the yoke of an imperious priefthood, they are abfolved from the obligations of religious authority. The ignorance once cherifhed by a defigning clergy is now operating the eftablifhment of national infidelity ; and the blood of martyred Huguenots has fallen upon the heads of thofe whom the convulfions of an empire has torn from the fanctuaries of their guilty authority.

Laftly. In the changeful fyftems of thefe triumphant anarchifts ; in the facility with which they diffolve the bonds of pledged allegiance, and fluctuate through all the varieties of government, will be read the formidable rifque which an empire incurs by the doubtful chance

of

of political experiment. When once the sinews
of a government are destroyed, and its ancient
forms are sacrificed to undiscriminating zeal,
not all the vigor of patriotic virtue, not all
the surviving energy of public spirit will be suf-
ficient to check the influx of licentiousness,
or inspire the enacted laws with effective authority. The powerful enthusiasm which accompanied this revolution was seen to dictate a
thousand refinements upon ancient policy, whose
practicability and expedience were never de-
bated.—In laudably detesting the horrors of
tyranny, they rushed into the full blaze of un-
bounded freedom, where, frantic with excess
of joy, they indulged in dreams of immaculate
policy, and awoke in the arms of a *faction*. It
was in this interval that wide destruction was
carried into all the departments of established
authority. Absolved from the control of ancient
laws, all orders were seen to blend in unwar-
rantable licence : the vigor which should coerce
being no longer felt, all the sluices of iniquity
opened upon the convulsed empire :—before its
impetuosity sunk the surviving reliques of di-
lapidated grandeur; and so large a portion of
Europe exhibited one extended scene of devasta-
tion and horror.

Amidst

Amidſt reflections of ſuch a nature, the mind cannot dwell without advantage; and leſſons of moſt ſalutary moment will not fail of impreſſing all ranks of poliſhed ſociety. If the dread decree of univerſal anarchy be not gone forth; if the waſting meſſengers of fate are not compaſſing the diſorganization of Chriſtian empires, the different orders of ſocial eſtabliſhment will perfect their wiſdom by the events which have now tranſpired, and conſolidate their authority by a ſyſtem of more perfect policy.

Magiſtrates will learn to venerate that law themſelves adminiſter, and to wield with diſcrete energy the ſceptre of authority.

Stateſmen will learn to inſpire their councils with equitable policy; to œconomize the fruits of national induſtry; to baniſh corruption from their adminiſtrative functions, and to exalt above every conſideration of intereſt and aggrandizement, the public good.

Nobles will learn to uſe with temper the privileges of their condition; to exert no wanton tyranny over the humble dependents of their

acci-

accidental influence, and to appear deferving of the honours they inherit by the dignified characteriftics of an exalted virtue.

The *Minifters of Chriftianity* will learn to purify the fyftems they teach from all the fictions of an interefted theology ; they will learn to guard againft the baneful confequences of imperious dogmatifm and fanctimonious fuperiority ; they will learn to diffufe the mild luftre of religious inftruction through the darkened fphere of ignorance and profligacy, and to beget in the public mind a growing veneration for the altars of national religion.

Laftly. The *Inferior Orders of Society* will acknowledge the magnitude of thofe calamities which Change produces, and learn to cultivate the unfafhionable virtue of political content : they will learn to regard, with juft eftimation, the folid advantages of a permanent authority, and tremble to break up that venerable foil out of which have flourifhed fuch generous fruit. Secure in the conftancy of liberal protection, they will dread to encounter the tumultuous hazard of a diffeated fovereignty ; and balancing the partial defects of a reigning fyftem

agun?

againſt the incalculable diſorders of a new-moulded authority, will ſuffer no deluſive doctrines to warp their loyalty, or ſophiſticate their patriotiſm. Thus will all orders participate of one common principle, and connect by motives of mutual intereſt in bonds of ſtricter union. The conſtitution will thus acquire a more compact ſtability, and its fainting ſprings receive a new energy ; fear will be ſupplanted by fidelity, ſubjection replaced by obedience ; the harmony of content will be amply extended, the influence of religion widely felt ; and the tranquillity of Europe will not have been broken in vain.

FINIS.

www.ingramcontent.com/pod-product-compliance
Lightning Source LLC
Chambersburg PA
CBHW032248080426
42735CB00008B/1047